Towards the Light

Catherine Rufnak

BookLeaf Publishing

Presentation by *BookLeaf Publishing*

Web: www.bookleafpub.com

E-mail: info@bookleafpub.com

ISBN: 9789395755153

First edition 2022

DEDICATION

To anyone traveling their own dark paths....

There is a light at the end of the tunnel

To Dallas and Jessica- thank you for being a good friend

ACKNOWLEDGEMENT

Usually people would have others to acknowledge in this section. I would like to acknowledge bookleaf publishing for giving me a chance to go outside my comfort box.

PREFACE

A journey through the dark and into the light of
a new beginning

What is Love

Love is seeing the smile on your face,
Love is feeling your warm embrace.

Love is thinking what you can do,
Love is always thinking about you.

Love is a feeling you get deep inside,
It brings out your hope, it shows us your pride.

Love is a bond that two people share,
It's a knowing that you'll always be there!

Love is a rose blooming in the spring,
Love is continuous just like a ring.

Love can't be forced, it can't even be fake,
Fake love can be your biggest mistake!

Tears

I have waited seven years.
Your a lion I have to take.
I am holding back my tears.

To look towards all my peers.
I watched and waited till they came.
I have waited seven years.

I look and see a lot of seers.
I am sorry; I will never be the same.
I am holding back all my tears.

People like to drink lots of beers.
Boys and girls love to play a game.
I have waited seven years.

I will conquer all my fears.
I will also get some fame.
I am holding back my tears.

Now I'm getting old my dears.
Just listen, the wind still blows your name.
I have waited seven years.
I am holding back my tears.

Ice Heart

They wind blows softly,
My hearts already chilled.

The year is flowing by so slowly,
Time is standing still.

My love for you has vanished,
Beneath the fading sky.

The earth seems to sleep,
As I sing my lullabye.

The time is getting closer,
The time that I shall leave.

My heart will change to ice,
As my body continues to bleed.

You Are

You are my life,
You are my soul.
You are the air that I breathe.

You are my hero,
You are my light,
You are everything I need.

You are my love,
You are my hope,
You are in my dreams.

I love you so much,
I will love you forever,
I will love you for eternity.

I want you to love me,
I want you to see,
I want you to help me whenever I need.

I want you to be honest, loyal and true.
But most of all,
I want you.

Why?

Why must I be different?
Why must I care?
Why must I love?
Things that aren't truly there.

Why must I run?
Why must I hide?
Why must I leave?
When I start to cry.

Why must I be left out?
Why must I hate?
Why do they leave?
Am I just second rate?

Why must I wonder?
Back through my dreams.
To both the joys and sorrows.
That they once did bring.

Some days I am happy!
Some days I am sad!
Why does everyone make me feel so bad?

Feelings

I sit in the window ledge, listening to the wind.

I hope and I dream, where should I begin?

It's hard to know where to stop!

I wonder if my life will just go pop.

I have made so many mistakes.

It's way more then I can handle.

It's way more then I can take.

I feel lost and I feel alone!

Night Time Prayer

The blade is sharp
My flesh is soft
They are such a perfect match.

Together they make a river of pain and joy
A knowing that I can feel
It brings me peace.

I watch the blood run down my arm
It only hurts briefly
Cut my cut my emotions are let out.

Bit by bit no more tears
I will be glad once the pain stops
If only to hear you whisper to me.

I love you and everything will be alright

But by then…

My blood will be shed
My life will be spent
My heart will be broken
I will be dead!

My Vows

I have spilt so many tears, it's a miracle that I
can cry.

I have had my heart broken so many times, it's a
miracle I even have one.

My soul has been shattered, it's a miracle it's still
intact.

You brought so much happiness into my life,
ever since I met you.

I can't believe it's starting to fade away.

We keep on accusing and blaming each other,
will it all end in pain?

I feel so lost, like I'm getting pushed away.

I have caused you so much pain, so why do you
let me stay?

My journey to find you took so long, I know it
wasn't a waste of time.

I love you and always will, I am yours but are you mine?

It hurts to know your trust in me is fading, that you just can't seem to believe.

It hurts that you choose to believe others over me.

My heart has been stolen by you, that's how it will remain.

Please just believe me… I am always going to stay.

Fighting for Life

The rushing of the water,
The thunder of the fall,
The calling of the ocean,
As I visit the sea floor.

The flashing of the lights,
The coolness of the air,
The blinding of the white,
As people look at stare.

The sharpness of the needle,
The bluntness of the knife,
The burning of the candle,
As they fight to save my life.

The stiffness of the table,
The silence of the night,
The sorrow of the family,
As they said I lost the fight.

The wetness of the tears,
The growing mourning call,
The crying of the century,
As my coffin begins to fall.

The tossing of the dirt,
The darkness all around,
The silence of the earth,
As I rest now underground.

Suicide

My tears fall freely now that I have let you go.
Don't hurt yourself because of my mistake.
Even though I am not with you any longer.
Doesn't mean we still can't be friends.

Maybe some where down the tracks,
We will be together once more.

I'm sorry I broke my promise to you.
I am now thinking which option would be best.

A knife, a rope, electricity with water?
Or
I will jump off a cliff like I so want to do.

Pain

The scars are getting deeper.
The blood is running free.
The pain is getting stronger.
Why won't you let me be?

My clothes are stained,
Red with blood.
As I fight to control the time.

The pain spreads faster,
I want it to end.
Tears flow down my cheeks.
I can't find a way to end it all.

A simple cut,
A painful thought.
That is all it takes.

A lost memory,
No more hope,
Leads dreams and faith astray.

Death

I pick up the knife, and smiled weakly to myself.

I let the blade run down my skin.

Soon words start to form as the blood drips down.

Soon this life will be over and I can finally be at peace.

I know no one will miss me.

I'm not special enough to be missed.

I hate it when I hurt others.

It's really hard to explain.

There is no point in living.

Life is just a game!

Believe Me

Would you believe me if I said I love you?
That I thought you were the one.

Would you open up to me?
Let me see you cry.

Would you be there to wipe away my tears?
Even if there were none.

Would you listen to my feelings?
That I have deep down inside.

Because...

I would believe you, when you say that you love
me.
That you think I am the one.

I would open up to you.
Let you see me cry.

I would be there to wipe away your tears.
Even if there were none.

I would listen to the feelings.

That you hold deep down inside.

I will do all this and more.
The reason for this, I will forever and always
love you.

True Love

I have made so many mistakes,
Maybe you just can't see.

I wish that I could fade away,
That this was all just a dream.

Every time I speak,
Something else goes wrong.

Is this all just one big lie?
Is it all just a game?
Was it my fault that your feeling this way?

I am sorry if your scared,
If your afraid of loosing me.

But I can promise you now,
You have nothing to fear.

I will always remain with you,
I will catch your tears.

I will love you till the end of time,
Further then the eye can see.

I am hurting deep inside,
Hoping you will stay with me.

I don't want to hurt you,
I don't want to make you cry.

It's hard to keep on seeing,
Through non clouded eyes.

Tears spill freely,
My cheese are long since stained.

I love you forever more,
That how it will remain!

Away

Away went the buildings,
Away went the noise,
Away went the life I lead,
The one I use to enjoy!

Away went the dreams,
Away went the tears,
Away went the family,
The one I held so dear!

Away went the laughter,
Away went the joy,
Away went the happiness,
Of every girl and boy!

Away went the music,
Away went the song,
Away went the tune,
The rhythm where I belonged!

Away went the sunshine,
Away went the rain,
Away went the wind,
Never to be seen again!

It's okay, not to be okay!

When it's dark and your alone
When the shadows start to die
When the twinkle of the stars fade to the
morning light.
When the sun burns so hot you can barely
breathe
Just know your not alone, that I am here if you
need.

When the earth does start to tremble
When you fall into the sea
When the waves all crash and tumble
When the world around you crumbles
Just know your not alone, that I am here if you
need.

When the air outside grows colder
When your body starts to numb
When the happiness disperses
When you feel the need to succumb
Just know that it's okay, it's okay to feel this
way. Just know it's ok to not feel okay.

Just know your not alone, just know that I am
here, just know that I have a shoulder and a
listening ear.

Mothers Love

Ten little fingers
Ten little toes
Two little eyes
And a button nose.

Two perfect ears
Two chubby cheeks
Rosie red lips
With smiles for weeks.

Two strong arms
Two long legs
A round little tummy
Filled with milk
That shows your fed.

Nine long months
I held you inside
Two short years
I carried you close
The rest of your life
I will be here

To hold you close
To comfort you

To love you
To protect you

My life changed when you came
My life now has meaning
You are my treasure
You are my son!

Storm

The wind outside is howling,
The sky has gone black.
The thunder in the clouds is rumbling,
The lightning starts to crack.

The rain starts to fall,
The hail buckets down,
The trees bellow in the wind,
The silence throughout the town.

The wind outside starts to slow,
The clouds start to break
The sun starts to shine through
The storm begins to shake

The light it starts to shine,
The colours start to show
A brand new hope awakens
With every bright and colourful rainbow.

Let it End

25

Let the knife cut sharp

Let the blade sink deep

Let the skin run red

Let the blood flow free

Let the numbness spread

Let the darkness creep

Let the breath grow cold

Let the heart miss a beat

Let the colour drain

Let the tears fall down

Let the time stand still

Let the life come to an end.

New Beginnings

The sun is slowly setting,
Along the eastern sky.

The day has finally ended,
A new beginnings nigh.

The black band of the sky,
The twinkling of the stars.

The night moves along so slowly,
But within the blink of an eye.

The sun is quickly rising,
The day has just begun.

A chance to start a new
To play and have some fun.

Live life to the fullest
Love with all your might.

For each new day,
Brings brand new ways
And beginnings from each Heart.

Eddys Tiger

This is written for my son:

My name is Eddy, and I have a secret.
Under my bed, and behind my toys.
I have a Tiger that makes no noise.

He is t like others, as he is green and red.
But, for some reason he likes it, under my bed.

It's dark under there, but every night.
My Tiger comes out and gives me a fright.
He doesn't mean to, he's pretty quite sneaky.

I have to admit, he is rather cheeky.
He sneaks to the kitchen, to get us some snacks.

Then in an instant he is sneaking right back.
A plate full of food, and a glass of warm milk.

Then back under the bed with his favourite quilt.
It's time for a nap, for Tiger and I.
So for now I must say, see you later...
Goodbye!

www.ingramcontent.com/pod-product-compliance
Lightning Source LLC
La Vergne TN
LVHW021335200726

843509LV00014B/2538